Afterimage

AFTERIMAGE

Poems by
Len Krisak

Measure Press
Evansville, Indiana

Copyright © 2014 by Len Krisak
All Rights Reserved
Printed in the United States of America
First Edition

The text of this book is composed in Baskerville.
Composition by R.G.
Manufacturing by Ingram.
Cover Design: R.G.

Krisak, Len
  Afterimage / by Len Krisak. — 1st ed.

  ISBN-13: 978-1-939574-06-0
  ISBN-10: 1-939574-06-4
  Library of Congress Control Number: 2013957221

Measure Press
526 S. Lincoln Park Dr.
Evansville, IN 47714
http://www.measurepress.com/measure/

Acknowledgments

I wish to thank the editors of the following periodicals. A number of the poems in *Afterimage* previously appeared in these titles, although sometimes in a slightly different form.

The Antioch Review: "Pentecost Accounting"
The Atlanta Review: "A Chicken with Its Head Cut Off"
The Boston Globe: "Discovery in the Renovation of an Underground Boston Subway Stop"
Buckeye: "1956 and 1959"
The Cortland Review: "Bath House"
Dappled Things: "Paper Napkins"
The Dark Horse: "Forty Years on, the Classicist Connects"
Dogwood: "Disproportion"
Fashioned Pleasures: "Feminine Endings"
The Formalist: "Paper Boy"
The Hopkins Review: "Restoration" and "To the Sessions"
The Hudson Review: "What Was Left"
Iambs & Trochees: "An Italianate Façade on the Boston Garden"
Lucid Rhythms: "Three Attitudes"
Margie: "At the New Bedford Museum" and "Kahlo's *Self-Portrait with Monkey*"
Measure: A Review of Formal Poetry: "Silhouette"
National Review: "A Hill in Massachusetts," "Construal," "Foyer," and "Verismo"
New England Review: "Advances in Endoscopy"
Peterloo Poets Prize Anthology: "Some Sounds"
Post Road: "Winter Exercises"
Red Savina Review: (As "Apothegms"): "Dedicated to PETA," "Didactic Poetic Precept," "Exhortation," "For Some," "No Thanks, Torso," and "To the Feminist Left in America"
Rosebud: "Intelligences"
The Sewanee Review: "Stranger with Evangels" and "Veteran Sub"
Stand Magazine: "Difficult"
The Valparaiso Poetry Review: "Conflation"
The Warwick Review: "Tie"
Writers' Haven Anthology: "Image," "Nearly Summer," and "Two Roads Diverged"

for Ruth

CONTENTS

Afterimage . . . xi

A Chicken with Its Head Cut Off . . . 1
Advances in Endoscopy . . . 2
A Hill in Massachusetts . . . 3
Allusive . . . 4
An Italianate Façade on the Boston Garden . . . 6
A Public Park in Springfield . . . 9
At the New Bedford Museum . . . 11
The Back of My Father's Head . . . 12
Bath House . . . 13
Borders . . . 15
Bound . . . 16
Conceit . . . 18
Conflation . . . 19
Construal . . . 20
Difficult . . . 21
Discovery in the Renovation of an Underground Boston Subway Stop . . . 22
Disproportion . . . 23
Elegy in a City Church-Scape . . . 26
Not in So Many Words: Epigrams . . . 28
Feminine Endings . . . 32
Fit for a Runner . . . 33
For the Critics, at His Death . . . 34
Forty Years On, the Classicist Connects . . . 35
Foyer . . . 37
Image . . . 38
Intelligences . . . 39

Kahlo's *Self-Portrait with Monkey*	40
Last Geranium	41
Lesson	42
Lyric	43
Nearly Summer	44
1956 and 1959	45
On *Jeopardy!*, the Make-Up Man	47
Paperboy	49
Paper Napkins	50
Pedestrian	51
Pentecost Accounting	52
Preserve	53
Restoration	55
Silhouette	57
Some Sounds	58
Stranger with Evangels	59
Three Attitudes	60
Tie	62
To the Sessions	63
Two Roads Diverged	65
Verismo	66
Veteran Sub	67
Watch City	68
What Was Left	69
Winter Exercises	70

Afterimage

Persistent in the camera of the eye,
Unwilling that its moving picture die,
The author of the image that it's made,
The figure lives its half-life. Must it fade?
Mind's palimpsest exploits the memory
Till waking dream imagines it can see.

A Chicken with Its Head Cut Off

It is a catch-phrase that she's never heard,
And yet the pullet knows just what to do:
The body zigzags, fakes, and jukes — a bird
In high-stakes tag. Around the yard she races,
As if she could elude the man who chases
With the hatchet still in hand, its blue
Steel filmed in red. His other hand has thrown
Away the head from which a clutch of bawks
Was wont to come. Intent, a small boy gawks.
It's not just what's for dinner that is known.
Life goes on — the ashy-feathered breast
And wings and legs. The sun sets in the west.
Here comes the upside-down, the useful, torso.
Now what he knows, the boy knows even more so.

Advances in Endoscopy

Sprouting wires that snake from seven leads,
She swallows it — a camera-pill that tumbles
Through her gut, *Fantastic Voyage*-like,
A lozenge lensing where intestine feeds.
Will there be blood? We wait. The science humbles.
A thousand shots fed through the pack she's strapped
To — cell phone-sized computer — tell him, "Strike
Here while the argon plasma's hot." All rapt
Before the screen, we look at where she bleeds,
Each pin-prick he intends to cauterize.
The capsule has become our tunnelers' eyes.
G.I., G.I. The letters drive us mad
To get back safely to the world we had.
The capsule's perfect signal fades, then dies.

A Hill in Massachusetts

The slope down which, come snow, beginners ski,
October hikers climb now with a will,
Trudging up trails to see what they can see
From crests that look out down the Great Blue Hill.
The work, against brown swathes of meadow grass,
Concludes when devotees at last attain
A top where white stones tower in a mass,
And, turtle-turned, a peeling dory's lain
Who knows how many years. How very strange!
A lighthouse and a stranded little boat,
Above the sea six hundred feet and change,
Where far peaks are the only things that float.
It is almost enough (which means it's not)
To make us think we stand on Ararat.

Allusive

> *But Ulysses . . . strung it as easily as a skilled bard strings a new peg of his lyre.*

Its mock-up of a Hopper oddly real,
The trolley grinds on downtown, sparsely-souled,
In sulphurous light (with tints of lemon peel
And feeble little rinds of grey and gold).

Once there, completing one of seven laps
(Or perhaps "closing yet another loop"?),
The train heads back. Straphangers hang by straps
(Or would, if any stood. Each head a drupe,

The zestless patrons sit.) Above them, strung
Up down the car, two rows of empty nooses
Dance to bouncing cross-ties. Loosely hung,
They jiggle to remind us of their uses.

Morbid speculation! Nothing here
Remotely hints of Nuremberg, strange fruit,
Or Ithaca — where slave girls slack with fear
But soon far tauter than a new-tuned lute,

Like thrushes snared as they come home to roost,
Twitched miserably (and in a fiction, too) —
Chicks dangling from a blind bard's "grimmer nest."
No, this is nothing like. The Hopper hue

Half-burnishes these riders mostly mum,
Which means few find their sentences cut short.

What feeble talk obtains admits the hum
Of trolley wheels. What is there to report

Except for febrile fancy run amok —
Imagination bootless in pursuit
Of sick suggestion that it cannot shuck?
The jaundiced light chokes off the day's commute.

An Italianate Façade on the Boston Garden

Around from staggered quoins
Locking the buff-and-butter-colored front and sides,
Down planes of which the dawn sun glides,
And on its public face, where mortar joins

The rusticated brick
To higher stories dressed in almost-ashlar stone,
The posh hotel has held its own.
Light plays on the entablature its trick

Of early-morning cream
Perversely sinking, washing down the curtain wall
To settle, in a silent fall
From penthouse heights, on pavements breathing steam.

Between the window rows,
The free hand of the architect still interposes
A line of bosses cast as roses.
On corbels made to seem like torches pose

Pineapples thrusting through
Split pediments the windows wear — and have so worn
For ages, long before were born
Those passers-by granted the current view.

Timeless as well, the swags
That drape some piers in catenaries, or festoon
The shallow niches now, as noon
Draws near, to lift the shade from sidewalk flags.

But light that melts and seeps
Its way — or tries to — deep inside this rich façade
(And bathes the visage of a god
Who looks perhaps Apollo-like, and keeps

His chin upon a dome
Of canvas standing in for what could be an awning),
And ever since the day's first dawning
Has warmed the masonry in monochrome —

How nearly may it come
To pattern how the spirit moves upon the forms
Of obdurate matter as it warms?
Might not our truest type be taken from

The model of that tower
Set down but barely half a city mile away
And clad in glass for pure display?
It cloaks itself in self-reflecting power,

Sans every ornament
But one, which serves to ward off all that might come near:
Bright, brittle panes where there appear,
Oh, little more than shapes in which are blent

The traffic of a day
And what it's spent. Should these machined and polished squares
That spurn whatever sunlight shares
Then represent, in silicates, our clay?

The meaning-making mind,
So prone to have its say no matter what we will,
May well elect stone's yielding still,
And come to rest on what has been designed

For radiance, surely:
That architrave, pilaster, console, and volute,
Amidst acanthus-tangled fruit,
Have mixed their blessing for us not obscurely,

But plain as each motif
May show. Though clearly not the palace of some Pitti,
It offers to this earthly city
A structure built once out of the belief

That though derivative,
Such forms and shapes embody both some fine ideal
And all the world should take for real,
Seen in the proper light where it must live.

A Public Park in Springfield

These zebra finches — nothing like their name,
But fawn and white — might make one think them tame,
So little do they evidence of fear.
Where is their finches' fright, now that *I'm* here,
Standing an arm's length from them? Not one flinches
Or flits when I extend my hand, mere inches
From fonts of cuttle latticed to the wall,
But cupped beneath a sky just twelve feet tall,
They peck away, each planted on his perch,
Domed under glass, as safe as if in church.
The tender ministrations of the state
Have netted them this separate, peaceful fate,
Wherein they never sow, but always reap,
Earning my wonderment, if not their keep.
Whose eye is sharper? Mine, to note the bright
Gold thorn they dip into the widow's mite
Of seed on which their few but fluttering needs
Depend? Or theirs, whose cool black pupil feeds
On me drinking them in? A bootless query,
Considering I see an aviary
Where they — who after all, should know, one trusts —
Perceive no absence of those gales and gusts
That stir the air outside this little dome,
But find themselves, oh, perfectly at home.
That being so, how cunning is the joke
On both of us that in its master stroke
Of — advertising? signage? nomenclature? —
The state has settled on this house of nature

The word *conservatory*, planting mums
And palms and orchids with its great green thumbs
Until the finch's hemisphere is filled.
(One, God has beaked; the other, man has billed.)
All right, a poor jest. Still, it recognizes
The tropes of separateness in all their guises:
Cut off from high blue rondure far beyond
The small finch knows no failure to respond;
Peace lilies see the light but take no air,
While bird and watcher look right through what's there.
A man upon whose head the hairs are numbered,
I leave the zebra finches unencumbered
Inside their microcosmos of the earth,
Alone aware of what this world is worth.

At the New Bedford Museum

Its dirty, bolted bones hang from a ceiling
That keeps *me* in suspense: some thirty tons
Over my head have sent the senses reeling
In apprehension, and the daring stuns.

Did no one doubt these cables, chains, and ropes
From which the blue whale's bones — and on which mine —
Depend? It would seem not. I hang my hopes
Mid-air, where, sixty-six feet long, the spine

Curves, like a sine compressed, through space that stands
For sea. Like ship propeller blades or bony
Petals, the sockets mock the fins of fans;
Their threaded pockets breach the creature's stony

Helmet, and drill the cord on through a skull
That splits to mimic two titanic shears.
(These look as thick and hard as any hull,
Despite their likeness to a brace of spears.)

The pincer ribs parenthesize in pairs,
Their only emphasis an emptiness —
Wind tunnel high above our stiff-necked stares
And full of airy nothing, more or less.

The blue whale in its blankness shoulders on,
Immobile mobile trussed up out of bone.
I wonder at my faith that what is gone
Remains; the skeleton swims on alone.

The Back of My Father's Head

It is a hurricane so tame, so mild,
Its iris is the widdershins of wild.
Fine silver circles to a tonsured eye,
While farther out, a pearl like early smoke
Counter-clocks to nacre by and by.
The thin hairs comma, each a pliant spoke
That yields before his wispy Slavic will.
And as pale charcoal ciliates a nape
Of ninety years, and settles to its shape,
The perfect little storm of hair stands still.

Bath House

Newton, Massachusetts

As twilight fizzles out, the last few glints
Off Crystal Lake, decanted, stake their claim
To one's attention: evanescent hints
That seconds will elapse before the same

Insipid slice of what must be the beach
Appears — stale, flat, and profitless by now.
(It's fall.) Into the cordoned shallows reach
The swimmers' docks, as far as signs allow.

The roped floats bob like corks, as from the train
One sees it loom: what made the city think
To name this structure after Gil Champagne,
Then, giddy with sheer drollery, paint it pink?

Patchy with peeling stucco, there it sits,
Its fundament approached by phlox and mums,
The Spanish roofline scalloped out in fits
And starts, the windows grilled, the sands like crumbs.

Drink it in quick, before these whimsies pass
Across the hurtling window pane, to melt
In shadow, and your visage ghosts the glass;
Before no civic summer can be felt.

Some after-image then, may draw you in,
And later rise with second thoughts in sleep,
Despite the way, in bed, you splash and spin,
Sensing the double vision of the deep.

Perhaps then, fear that tingles there in dream,
Or laps like waves at waking's tilted rim,
Will bubble up and break, and make it seem
The troubling world will yield itself to whim.

Borders

Nearly bent in half, he found his way,
Crab-like, across the floor of the café,
Then docked his backside in a beat-up chair.
His kowtow posture lent the man an air
Of one inspecting, microscopically,
The table for such germs as he could see,
Or falling to a draftsman's close perusal.
The coffee brought him met with no refusal,
For he loudly slurped it inches from
The surface, tipped, and once more through a scrum
Of chairs went scuttling, doubled over, not
With laughter but the burden of his lot.
Where cheap whodunits stretched in endless lines,
I saw him shortly after, eyeing spines.

Bound

Gilding the train car walls with its declension,
Another of those gliding autumn suns
Begins to go, so slow its slanted rays
Seem counter-tokens of that bright suspension
The poet says can't last. Gold never stays?
Perhaps. But notice, as the trolley runs

For Riverside, that young man with his nose
Inside a book whose cover — *Learn Inglès!* —
Suggests an author's eye that gleamed with wit
Once. Follow, as an index finger flows
Across the page to con some strange new phrase.
Who knows what he may someday make of it?

See how his brow will knit and then un-knit?
New to the Green Line and its rattling ways,
He has to find his place at every jolt.
But with intensity that will not quit,
He perseveres like some insistent colt.
A golden pupil with a laser gaze,

The boy has failed to notice that we're there
(I mean, that we have reached our final stop).
Clearly, the words have left him in a daze,
Their power hardly that of beauty bare
(Since stripped-to-marrow grammar rarely pays
Unless one's learning "thanks" or where to shop).

But something in those pulp-grade leaves has held
Him till the train's inevitable arrival.
As he steps off, that yellow gouache still paints
Our car, the light a honeyed coat of geld,
The walls washed in the haloed gold of saints,
The sight forever ambered in survival.

Conceit

Over the side, a window washer stands
Up on his lifeboat scaffold, thirty floors
Above the sea of people down below.
The davits on the roof deck, to commands
We cannot hear, are lowering away,
The progress, as it must be, more than slow.
He makes his way sans benefit of oars,
Stupendously alone descending day,
Until he comes to what must be the whim
Some sea-drunk architect once drew: a row
Of portholes puncturing the stone façade.
He leaves each spyglass pane shipshape and trim,
In on the joke he knows is not on him,
But aimed instead at some titanic god.

Conflation

Sometimes through atomizing mist, or now
And then from deep within a muffling fog's
Opacity, there will appear three dogs
In placid trot, each leading, free of strain,
Their mistress by a leash, to teach her how
To run in autumn-winter morning dark.
And though I've never heard a warning bark,
(They are so used to me, and to her rein),
Still, they announce their slow epiphany
By jangling collar bells, as they (and she)
Emerge, developing a photograph,
Which prints, through sleet or baths of grainy snow,
An image half from ancient myth and half
From frozen steppes. Then, on the foursome jogs.
Well, all of us have somewhere we must go.

Construal

Poised on the trolley's stair step lip, he tenses,
Shooting, from time to time, an anxious look
Down the converging tracks. Where is his stop?
A tremor seems to commandeer his senses,
Shaking the OJ quart his armpit's nook
Pins hard against him; nothing's going to drop.

In flannel Stewart plaid he barely tucks
In Carhartt pants, his figure makes one figure
Him for local, but if that's so, how come
His green and purple baseball cap says *Bucks*?
What makes him make one think him like a trigger?
What's that between his finger and his thumb?

Could it just be a Lucky Strike (unlit,
Of course), since in the other hand, he grips —
The way one holds a detonator; see? —
His Bic, impatient to get off with it,
As if there waited at his fingertips
The signaling device from *Jeopardy!*?

Difficult

Now they lay me down to strap
me in. I pray they keep my spit
I curse them with from off the gurney.
Incontinently comes the crap
I give them as I give them shit
and give them blood and tears.
Ninety years, and this is where the journey
ends, sans sons. It's ninety years,
and there she is, but then she goes,
which makes it take three men to hold me down.
Don't ever leave me all alone.
The nurses and the nurses' aides
and everybody in the corridor — they gawk.
I'm nothing but my thrashes and my throes.
They threw me through the plate glass; shards and blades
prickle from my skin. I'd watch them like a hawk
if only they would let me.

Come and get me.

Discovery in the Renovation of an Underground Boston Subway Stop

White tiles, their serifs kerned like leveled spears,
Have formed in ranks of Roman capitals:
ARLINGTON. Laid in here a hundred years
Ago, they dignify these dirty walls
With stately gravitas, their borders coped
In black. So far, no vandal's hand has X'd
Them out, or left their chaste decorum groped.
Graffitists still have not defaced the text,
Tagging its letterforms. The modern crew
Remodeling this station of the "T"
Have yet to figure out what they should do.
Air-hammers leave the word for all to see
For now, mosaics worthy of a Rome,
A ruined Ravenna, or a catacomb.

Disproportion

An outdoor exhibition of giant insect sculpture

Too dull to note what human hands or eyes
Framed symmetry from cedar, willow, teak,
I only dazzle at the monstrous size:
Bigger than *Them*, this hardwood ant's a freak

Of art, the locust gantry-legged, at least.
Each varnished carving guards a likely path:
The spider by the entrance, at his feast;
The monarch in a florid aftermath.

Ladybugs sit politely, big as domes
Come down to earth, while damselflies extend
Their fuselages through the aerodromes
Of birch and oak that seem to never end.

(With snowshoe wings their maker scaled to fit
The feet of any Bunyan or colossus,
These great zygoptera will never flit;
Three long feet wide, each wing spans a molossus.)

The praying mantis bows his head (to see us
As we see *him*, the pamphlet guide suggests?).
Inspecting insects, would he want to be us
If he could find our less than pious nests?

Like pods in Tootsie-Rolls, the dragonfly's —
Brown segments of a British bomber's body
(The Avro Lancaster's) that terrifies
By lengths it's gone to. Nothing here is shoddy

In teak articulated perfectly
With walnut polished to a blinding sheen.
The workmanship is faultless, one can see,
Though little jokes (what could the sculptor mean —

The grasshopper is carved from locust wood!)
Insinuate themselves at certain sites:
Carpenter ants by carpenters — that's *good*:
Admitting that we've got him dead to rites,

A humble and abashed assassin bug,
Head tucked so deeply in his thorax that
You'd think he's searching earth to find a rug
To pray on. Poison rostrum folded flat,

He jabs at meals ten times his size (it takes
Barely four seconds for their guts to melt),
Then sucks as if they were vanilla shakes.
It makes me think how dinner might have felt,

To realize that eating on that scale
Implies a hundred feet of poisoned prey.
He loves his ants, and yet his hollow nail
Of toxins floats there, only yards away.

More mutant species out of sci-fi circa
The fifties guard the dark wood on the way.
Late afternoon begins to drape its burqua
Over the trees and trails, shadowing day,

Driving me from the garden and its giant
Tropes of sculpted-out-of-timber creatures.

Expulsion finds me totally compliant,
Lest late tonight, I see once more their features

Looming, looming — all huge with blind intent.
But what do their feelers mean? There, I'm blind, too,
Dreaming of visions of what might be meant.
I wait . . . which seems the least that I can do.

Elegy in a City Church-Scape

First Baptist Church, Boston

Ninth-story balcony, much thanks for these
Reliefs drawn by their celebrated draughtsman
Bartholdi (and his deft Italian craftsmen).
I stare across the way, scanning the frieze:
At the square tower's carved out corners blow
Four chiseled trumpets long since free from gilt
(Four pouting angels pucker, too, of course,
As if to tout what Richardson has built,
But are they Gregory's, as they smile like angels
Who've forever cornered all the angles?
They puff through puddingstone, as if to force
Some note to warn the traffic snarled below,
Which toots its own horn, so to speak). McKim
Apprenticed to this church's architect,
Helping to elevate its seraphim
Almost two hundred feet — like the elect
Who swell the progress round its four square faces,
And in that path their pilgrim footsteps trace,
Trudge through the Christian's sacramental stages —
Baptism, Communion, Marriage, Death — to grace
The golden vista lent my vantage place
By fading light. (I watch this as it traces
Visages down which blue shadow washes,
Responding to day's melting, ochred phages
No moment stays.) The leveraged sunrays' gouaches
Model the models for these figures: saints,
One must suppose, who posed before Bartholdi
Only in his mind's eye: Garibaldi;

Hawthorne; Emerson; LaFarge; Longfellow;
Lincoln. Each marches on as sunset paints
Their edifice a certain slant of yellow.
Are these my trained binoculars playing tricks
That cannot pick out Lincoln? If he walks
The dark side of the church, where better angels
Anthem, I cannot seem to get a fix,
But speculate on what the spirit balks
At: is this side I see the site of christening,
And Lincoln subtly missing from Baptism-
By-fire of the nation? Who is listening
Now, or little noting, long remembering?
Now, nothing's left of all those credal wrangles
And their invitations to a schism.
This church's botched acoustics meant the end
Of services, suspended shortly after
Its consecration. Nothing billows, embering.
What mattered then, an object now of laughter
(The doctrine of Victorians defeated),
Stone stands protected by no partisans
But these gone round the tower's rectangled bend.
Over their heads, the spaced out bartizans
Project like prows on seas of faith receded.
What has this monument left to defend?
Its dark machicolations echoes of
The narrow oylets and the arrow slits
Of mighty fortresses, First Baptist sits,
A columbarium the brooding dove —
Unholy pigeon now, *zeit*-weary *geist* —
Haunts only as a roost from which it shits.
Abandoning the figures I have Zeissed,
I cord those glasses: time to stow away.
The vesper tolls the knell of parting day.

Not in So Many Words: Epigrams

Toppsed

Why is each morning's paper so damned trying?
The men on boyhood's baseball cards are dying.

Onegin in His Dotage

Back, back he drifts, consumed by that which he must rue:
A bullet and a ballroom and a billet-doux.

Dedicated to PETA

A lot of furry creatures like to roll in dung,
Then steal and kill the broods of others.
A lot of species like to eat their young.
So many mammals make such lousy mothers.

For Some

Not even ninety years of feckless drift
Can keep the end from seeming far too swift.

Didactic Poetic Precept

First astonish,
Then admonish.

Exhortation

Old Pegasus I've ridden for so long,
I beg you, help me put not one foot wrong.
Step slow enough to keep your rider humble,
And smartly when you sense me start to stumble.

No Thanks, Torso

Though I've been told to change my life by Rilke
(Be *better*? Pulse with human kindness' milke?),
I'm sorry, but I'm just not of that ilke.

To the Feminist Left in America

Be grateful you don't live in some Arabia.
Their patriarchals sew up women's labia.

Two Apophthegms on Passion

Far banks desire;
Near snuffs the fire.

Not the flesh
With which you choose
    To thresh,
      But *whose*.

Vow of Silence

Why else would I bite my tongue in sleep
Except that I have promises to keep?

Epigram out of Rome

Wandering this garden statued with Priapus,
That *three* eyes follow us does not escape us.

Fly-Over Teaser:
Which Is More Exotic?

The alien tracts of Madagascar
Or the backyard tracks of NASCAR?

On a Certain Maestro
Who Claims His Work Is Non-Political

Who on a podium
Deserves more odium?

Culture

Once more bullied to a standing O,
He asks himself, "Well what do *I* know?"

Feminine Endings

Picture her photographed, but never painted —
Plainly the object of a common passion
With which more than a few have been acquainted,
And to which some have been true in their fashion.
Some saw her head thrown back, her grey eyes rolling;
Few knew how to avert the gorgon gazes
Through which she saw her way to their controlling.
But more than all of this, what still amazes
Is all the hatred that her looks created.
So many fell into a trance, a doting,
They never knew when they had been defeated
By glances meant for them . . . but good for nothing.
So all of those who'd thought to take their pleasure,
Consoled themselves with spoils, and not with treasure.

Fit for a Runner

The wall and ground's hypotenuse, he leans
In hard, with palms against the stone, this boy,
As if he'd push it over: an Achilles
Stretch that looks as if its straining means
That block by block, he plans to press on till he's
Overthrown the topless towers of Troy.

For the Critics, at His Death

James Merrill, 1926-1995

Now Ephraim, come draw him near; refresh his
                    Soul with light.
O priceless Jim, they said you were "too precious."
                    They were right.

Forty Years On,
the Classicist Connects

It is a proposition much suspect
That when the editors (and what were they
But what teens were in 1964
In Michigan?) decided to select
His yearbook legend it was meant to pay
Homage either to Ronny Fairbanks or

To Horace. Mind you, there were Latin classes,
But those who ran the show — the pretty clique
Of queen and court; the smarter preppie jocks —
Were climbing something other than Parnassus.
The volumes that that tag line had to speak
Demanded English clearly strange yet heterodox:

"Oh, gather up the faggots while you can."
Incredibly, Book III, Ode 17:
"Dum potes, aridum / compone lignum,"
Though sans the *dry*. Beneath his image ran
Ronny's achievements: none — the white space seen
As confirmation; taken for a *signum*

Of nothing come from nothing. Mrs. Dohrn —
Two years from out to pasture, clueless, prone
To nodding off — was less than no defense
Against the small guffaws, the flippant scorn.
But Ronny Fairbanks left that crowd alone,
Sensing that if he showed he took offense,

There'd be no end . . . or worse. Impassive, stoic,
Stolid, he sprayed the produce down at closing
(I was a sacker at the Super-D).
Nothing done there was in the least heroic:
Not sweeping up; not Ronny's silent hosing;
No words from me to him, from him to me.

All intercourse between us in abeyance,
Suspended in the halftone standing in
For amber for forever till this day
Of classical translation and conveyance,
I look him in the eye and then begin.
Flaccus the pagan sings, "Be blithe; be gay."

Foyer

What are the houses of the old?
Last vestibules we enter,
Small vastnesses. They smell of mold,
Of camphor, and of must,
And of necessity, their center
Cannot hold.
Moth-eaten are their rooms
Where merely breathing dooms
Us to incorporating dust,
And to the anterooms that take us in.
Penultimately cold,
We wait there to begin.

Image

Between the *SUN* and oh, a great big *O*
(Both blue): one giant scarlet arrow like
A stickpin not quite showing through. It hides
Behind a yellow shield whose neon glow
Would seem to light a target one could strike
With godlike ease, and yet this thing elides
The shaft from blood-red tip to carmine nock.
Could Cupid's aimlessness have been so blind?
Or was some deadly joke instead Apollo's,
With us the pair that archer meant to mock?
Bewildering, what logos bring to mind:
We taunt the gods, but Ovid knows what follows.
You loved that sign, at twilight, in the snow,
In Philly, half a million years ago.

Intelligences

for Anthony Lombardy

Because it seemed to some that he was slow,
Or smiled too much at many simple things,
One might have thought him dumb. It was not so.
The way one waits for what the mailman brings,
We listened for his step and watched that door
That said his overcoated form was back
From where he went when we were five and four.
We saw that he had more than just a knack
For lifting us aloft or playing horse.
Both broad of back and smarter than a whip,
My father never took a college course.
And yet, I learned his learning was my light
By kissing, like a bird who bent to sip,
The stubbled cheek he'd turn to me each night.

Kahlo's *Self-Portrait with Monkey*

Two — make that one — black brow atop the eyes
Is flying through her forehead like a crow,
As if those temples were the slashed-on skies
Or wheat fields of that canvas by van Gogh.
Smudge-thick, this doubled-over wing. It rhymes
With thinner, finer lines of jet-black lashes
Mocking, like some coquette's — a set that mimes
In turn, still-finer, philtrum-cut mustaches
Faintly fading into the wings. Not quite
A sneer, obtruding from her upper lip,
Recalls the supercilious bird whose flight
First caught our eye, then snapped off like a whip.
With Charmin-package eyes dyed raven black,
The monkey gapes to see us staring back.

Last Geranium

Through overcast gun-metal gray,
At twilight fading fast away:
One hot pink petal in a pot,
Fired like Turner's pistol shot.

Lesson

Shallow to deep, we line the pool, with hands
On skinny hips, akimbo-armed: some shy,
Some bratty boys, who eye him as he stands
Erect, the low board quivering. Small fry
Of nine, what do we know of sights like these?
He's peeled his Speedo off and tried to sink
It for "a diving target." Each boy sees
His swimming teacher fail. What should we think
Of this — and all his thick, black, curly hair?
We stare hard at the suit — a soggy rag —
But not at him, a bare-but-shaggy bear.
Despite the knotted flesh, his shoulders sag.
With shame? Chagrin? Embarrassment? Regret?
No lotus of an answer floats up yet.

Lyric

Flat-out stretching flat without a will,
The plains do nothing to deserve that name
That they deserve. The drifting prairie grass
Goes on for miles that do not seem to pass.
Sifting the wind, the countless hours fill
The gaze with perfect nothing-but-the-same;
Nothing but the ruler-straight horizon —
The nothing that is there to fix the eyes on.

Nearly Summer

At five A.M. there is a bird — a crow —
Who everywhere, and all year long, says now
My rest is done; he says that I should know
The light's come on and he will show me how,
By cawing-in the dawn, the time's gone past
When I might hide in sleep or lie in wait.
He says the crucial moment's come at last
And that I cannot let the light grow late.
This raucous crow would be some common bird
Except that he has lighted in the tree
From which he knows his warning will be heard
Each morning, sure the light is meant for me.
He is so bold in what his voice commands,
He must believe this sleeper understands.

1956 and 1959

Our setting? Guess. Men still wore soft-brimmed hats
And Superman had helped to crush a Reich —
Which few thought odd. The TV's king of cats
Was Kellogg's Tony, Battle Creek liked Ike,
And Sugar Frosted Flakes straight from the box
Were *grrreat!* when doting kids got home from school
In time to watch the show that set their clocks.
In black and white, the Man of Steel would duel
With two-bit, cardboard bad guys known as crooks.
George Reeves wore out a union suit of blue,
And, corseted within his own good looks,
Whistled the cloudy air through which he flew.
World Capital of Cereal, the town
Survived on Kellogg's, Ralston's, Post's largesse —
So much that Clark Kent played not quite the clown,
But TV pitch man under fame's duress.
That's how it came to pass that Reeves, bedraped
In flannel, limo'd through our town on tour,
Grey mufti free of muscle pads that shaped
Him, as a rule. Well, we were kids, and sure,
At every school that set us free to crowd
A playground curb, that we should scan the sky.
Did we disturb him with our cry so loud
We could not hear him mouth the reason why,
When from the chauffeured Caddy dark he stepped
To smile and wave and say he could not fly
That day? That day, our bird-like hearts had leapt,
And then began — a bit — to learn to die.

Well, all right; whose must not? Two large bare hands,
Hooked in his grin, would bend no bars of steel.
One "super whistle" for his little fans,
And, prisoned in the awful image real
To children only, back he ducked. The car
Crept on toward other cheering scholars out
Of jail for just this feckless repertoire
Leading to nothing less than reckless doubt.
He fled, time flew, till one day in L.A.,
Reeves, slower than a speeding bullet, dead
In bed, had shaped us one last feat of clay.
A suicide, *Variety* had said.
And in our own *Enquirer and News*,
The faintest whiff of scandal — drink, The Mob,
Some woman. What were we to think, whose views
Had been of deeds that made small pulses throb?
Come down to earth with powers far beyond
The powers mortal men possessed, one actor —
"Trapped in the role" that like a cape he'd donned —
Came up against his final malefactor.
They said he burned the hair shirt suit each season's
End, when the shooting stopped. They said he grew
To hate the stupid stunts. Oh, he had reasons
To leave that show, and one day, we did, too.

On *Jeopardy!*, the Make-Up Man

His name was Dick who waved me to the chair
Where every man that day would joke and blush.
Three mirrors on the wall said, "You're not fair,"
But even to the homely it's a rush,
This being fussed at, feeling pampering hands
Applying pancake — even if a man's.

Dick brushed my cheek, soft bristles swishing hard,
Then patted at the temples flushing pink.
Paraded from the Green Room under guard,
I saw him bringing up our rear, from clink
To klieg lights. Pausing on the stage's lip,
I waited for my cue and failed to trip.

The audience assumed its proper hush,
I took my place and slowly piled up cash,
While Dick stood in the shadows' purple plush.
I "wagered" soberly — oh, nothing rash —
Until commercial break. Dick wheeled his cart
To Alex first, administering his art.

He flicked that star with one pale, powdery wisp,
Endured the stage director's snide remark,
Then trundling to me, whispered with a lisp,
"Oh, this is nothing. Smile!" Catching his spark,
I smiled, but couldn't say a single word
(The rules). Suppose someone official heard?

In fact, what Dick did could have cost his job
(We weren't allowed a wink, a word, a nod
With anyone). He spoke to me with swab
And puff and pad; I did not find it odd.
Tape ran again, and Dick was in the dark,
If there were need. We both had left our mark.

Ten years. I watched the show the other night
(Let's say, because it happened to be on).
Then credits crawled till all were out of sight
Who'd played their part. Dick's name and hands were gone.
Another rule: you can't go back again —
A fact I've thought of many times since then.

Paperboy

Worn down by words all afternoon, and all
Those words a toxic stream of pride and bile
And bitterness, while snow began to fall,
Settling outside the windows steamed with vile
Reproaches, there I thought how, when a boy
Out on my route, fresh snow seemed like relief
Almost from cold that froze the flesh. I'd toy
With flakes upon my tongue in the belief
That they would somehow warm me from within.
Trudging from door to drift-defended door,
I worked my way back home — and you'd begin.
I'd listen till I could not any more
Back then. Today, I plead to take a walk
Out in the gentle snow that cannot talk.

Paper Napkins

Roof-gardened twenty stories up, a brace
Of rays goes skating in bedeviled air
As if the wind were morning's hidden leaven.
They billow with a manta's nervous grace,
Then drop to break-dance, each a bright white square
Blown up and open to the sight of heaven.

Look how they roll and surge, then snap like sails,
Or carpet-ride the broad daylight, wild ghosts
Cut out of paper. Sometimes, both go stiff
A second, mimicking two chalice veils
That cover absence. Subject to the gusts
(Rehearsing *caper, hover, maybe, if*),

One pair of partners even when they're odd,
They lift themselves by random currents, whirl
Together, fly apart, but make no noise
Not sanctioned by their blind Aeolian god.
It is as likely they will reef as furl
At any given moment, like the toys

Of chaos loosed — mere playthings swirled around
Until some calm falls out of nowhere sensed
And seems to think that what has stopped must stay.
Then comes the whirlwind to which both are bound.
The napkins rise as called, and are dispensed
With, swept up, up, up, up, and then away.

Pedestrian

Straight out of "Trouble": Robert Preston's hands.
Head-high, they wobble like The Music Man's
In warning: DANGER! Lurching from the curb,
A marionette whose parts are purest verb,
He steps off Bolger-scarecrow-like toward Oz
(The other side). It gives us drivers pause
To watch a walk so far outside the norm,
Yet *traffic*'s being held up, *not* this form
Negotiating four lanes all alone,
So why hands-up? The street now all his own,
He staggers with a holy-roller's glee,
A spastic, touchdown-signalling referee
Who wig-wags us he'll soon be where he may
Walk on, hands-down, and we can pull away.

Pentecost Accounting

This gifted dove looks down on us in flames.
He condescends with blazing presence: words
That lick and scorch; that sear our tongues' twelve names.
Breath flickers like a torch song from this bird's
Now coal-white soul. Our frozen lungs, he stings.
See how those hearts turned upside down now hang
Their fire over us? The pigeon screams;
We burn beneath him. Those are bellows-wings
Blowing a love that singes skin. He seems
A tungsten god. Fire tastes like fear. The gang
We are, we were not then. We're not the same,
Speaking *lingua franca*. In fields far-flung,
We'll talk what's asked us, mouth a Roman tongue,
And stalk Damascus, un-Babeling His name.

Preserve

Gut-deep inside an exhibition hall:
The *Lesson in Anatomy by Tulp*,
Thrown on a screen before a black-dropped wall.
One cannot take it in in just one gulp,

It looms so large. Its *camera* not quite
Obscura gapes out at museum space
Where danglers posture in the gimlet light
And hangers-on, to keep a hard-won place

In line, must scrimmage in slow motion. *SOLD
OUT*, banners blazon to the busy street,
While puppeted in poses they will hold
Forever, opened up in indiscreet

And flagrantly revealing attitudes,
Mere bodies — wired, expertly filleted —
Confront us as a hundred visceral nudes.
A vengeful god's been here, and Marsyas flayed

Five-score. That plastic man we viewed as boys
(They sold *him* as The Visible) could never
Stand up to this German surgeon's ploys
(Since millions view the sinews that he's severed,

With bones and veins and eyes like devilled eggs).
How salmon-hued each teased-out muscle group!
And when one looks between so many legs,
How racked the genitalia that droop

Like scallops seined, or pink morels strung out.
But whether batter, ballerina, or
Suspended soccer player posed to tout
The virtue in these tissues leeched of gore

(And every single mortal fluid), all
Sport tasteful little silver artist's plaques
Appropriating carcasses with gall,
Which, oddly, every pickled body lacks.

Some say that *CSI* is hard to swallow;
That where the camera zooms, they dare not follow.
These gape at what the anger of Apollo
Yields when tamed: a hungry maw gone hollow.

And then the lines file out by twos and threes,
Worming their way through peristaltic stiles
And modeling intact anatomies
Whose faces feature somber human smiles.

Restoration

The sort of photo glimpsed in checkout lines
(Staring an act at which politeness frowns —
Or used to), features speak in telltale signs.
The brow the surgeon built, although this sounds

A bit bizarre, supports two light brown bridges
That don't go very far; they span a pair
Of only barely mismatched orbits' ridges,
Though, and add some contrast to her hair.

Why should the left eye, winking to a slit,
Look right but not look right, as if askance —
As if to ask why nothing's wrong with it
(The right)? Didn't the mastiff have his chance

At that as well? Her philtrum veers a tad
Off kilter, true — a bit off true, but not
Bit off. She has, if not the face she had,
The face that must resign her to her lot.

Off-center, too: the dragged-down lip that pouts
Almost, as if in some dubiety,
Unlikely as this might appear. Such doubts
About these grafts and their propriety

As she may entertain — if there are any —
Are anybody's guess. Perhaps such issues
Should be debated by the faceless many,
A subject (human tissue) fit for tissues

And organ swells and TV talking heads,
While she gives thanks that someone playing God
Attached her to this mesh of blushing reds
Her mirror still finds only slightly odd.

Silhouette

How still can one dog stand and still be dog?
This stationary shape provides a clue.
For through the mist that longs to be a fog,
The shaggy figure that some artist drew
And jig-sawed for a plywood golf-course guard
Says, "Not that long, unless, like mine, its form
Is flat against the groundhog's sky — and hard."
Though two dimensions aren't this creature's norm,
They seem to do: the rough is smooth; the greens
Run true, without a sign of rub or glitch.
Into the dawn, pure constancy, he leans
His profile; see the fixed intent with which
He poses, steadfast above the bunker sand,
Pointing out just how still one dog can stand.

Some Sounds

It was the polished hardwood floors, I think.
If someone in his socks slid overhead,
Then she was being chased. My heart would sink,
And then we'd hear what we had come to dread:
A thumping, sounding almost batting-muffled;
His voice's barking bass; her high thin scream.
That we agreed to say that they had *scuffled*
Just would not do. We knew that — it would seem —
And yet our silent pact was never broken:
Kim ran in vain; we listened to her sobs,
Her halting English stopped where fists had spoken.
Each day, we held our tongues and did our jobs.
This was when things were different, of course,
A good six years before our own divorce.

Stranger with Evangels

That it was shady made it easier,
It seemed, the summer morning not so bad
Beneath broad maple, oak, and elm. We had
A hundred flyers each, he said, "So run!"
(A task that now is no more than a blur,
Worth fifty cents when both of us were done.)
We never really read, so never knew
What dispensation we'd been heralds to,
But left his news on every porch and stoop,
Delivering unawares. God knows what group
Or cult or sect was paying what we earned;
Our father did not ask us what it taught,
And even stranger still, we never learned,
Had dimes been candy, what he would have thought.

Three Attitudes

It's not so much that *he* should be there, but
That anyone at all would want to haunt
This barren stage set of the underground.
Outwaiting trolley doors (when will they shut?),
He signals his intent to stay. Long, gaunt,
And young, he means to say he won't be bound

Somewhere; that he is proud to stand disheveled,
Intent in his inspection of . . . the *wall?*
Oh, *that's* it. There's a *map*, and to his side,
A glazed, green poster that the "T" has leveled
At its patrons: "Tahiti — Heed the Call."
Palms beckon like a waving travel guide.

As if he'd draw the map from smell alone,
Its legend and its color scheme transformed
To scent, he stands his ground so close, the nose
He's wielding barely seems to be his own.
And in a stance to which he's clearly warmed,
He roots there, striking a deliberate pose.

But then the trolley brakes release, their hiss
The signal that some curious charm is broken,
And like a top spun by a furious jerk,
He wheels to glare back at the half-cracked glass
As if some savage thing inside has woken.
He paints the glassed-in paradise a smirk,

Threatening its blandishments with half a sneer
And one whole non-existent javelin.
Then having mimed a man of menaces
With his imaginary brandished spear,
He freezes in the posture of that sin
For which God banished Cain in *Genesis*.

The train pulls out, abandoning this one-
Act playlet with its desolate platform stage,
Its doubtful climax, and its fearsome star,
Whose frozen bearing hints that it will run
No longer than his strength can match the rage
And terror burning in his repertoire.

Tie

The suit was bad enough. (It drove her mad
To think a son of hers would choose to wed
In shades of grey — especially Glen Plaid.)
But worse by far, the tie: solid maroon
He said he wasn't married to — a joke
That only seemed to make things worse. She said
It almost made her wish that she was dead.
The tie? The smart remark? That day in June,
She started crying fiercely, fit to choke.
The sobs that racked her came between wild gasps
And gulps. She never quite regained control,
And yet the rite came off without a hitch.
Something there was eluded both their grasps
That day, for though he never called her bitch
(Or she, him, S.O.B.), he set his soul
Against that day to come he should have seen,
When she would not be able to recall
Her name, much less what all of this might mean
And ties would matter little, if at all.

To the Sessions

Concatenated by whatever links
Us here, we sit and stand and pace and wait —
The mopers and the sighers and the fretters.
No doubt some drove after too many drinks.
A certain few bear papers for their date.
One rolls his eyes beneath the broken letters

Hand-stenciled on some isinglass, oh, long
Ago. Pure tedium attaches to
The afternoon that drags on in this hall,
As someone hums the fag-end of a song
My meager memory finds no matches to.
The lot of us await a trooper's call

By last names he will mispronounce just once.
How sorry are we that we're missing work,
I wonder, deeming us some band of brothers.
But that's the lazy daydream of a dunce,
I realize; why should the district clerk
Confuse my plight with that of all these others?

That's when one bored soul rises from the bench
Where he's been sitting, judging of the ceiling,
To shuffle off in shackles I have missed.
A cell-phoned crew cut gives his arm a wrench,
As both step out, a pair half-unappealing.
The young one in the silver cuffs looks pissed.

They're headed for the cooler or the can,
I see, to answer *one* of nature's calls.
They stop; the cop lets Manacles drink first,
As if the need were greater for a man
Who might be staring soon at three hard walls.
Till now, I have not guessed his raging thirst

(He gulps as if his need would set him free,
Chained to himself, but far from all abettors).
And as I hear a weak attempt to force
A version of my name, I rise, and see
Him bent above the fountain in his fetters,
Still drinking deeply from its bubbling source.

Two Roads Diverged

But what was yellow wasn't woods. She sat
With a Manhattan twirled between her thumb
And index finger, trading chit for chat,
Then sipped, leaned in, and smiled, striking him dumb:
"I want to get to know you *really* better."
Now all was clear — the booth, the "harmless" drink
Away from work. She wanted him? Well, let her!
But then . . . he thought the thought he'd longed to think:
A six-years wife, but wife only in name.
How could her hurt compare to pain like his?
This way meant things would never be the same
Again. He bolted down his sloe gin fizz,
One for the road. It's been a long time since,
But giving in's meant all the difference.

Verismo

Gentile Bellini, Constantinople, 1480

Perhaps this fits in some Vasari-like
Apocrypha? Sultan Mehmet II,
They say, presented by Bellini with
An oil of John the Baptist's severed head,
Repined: the painting wasn't true to life —
A blunt critique Bellini hadn't reckoned
On. So Mehmet ordered up a strike
One hopes was surgical (this may be myth):
A slave's neck was presented to a knife,
And afterward, the slave was truly dead.
No mention if the great Bellini shook,
Told "this is how a severed head should look."
Perhaps the captious Sultan meant no menace,
But Bellini soon returned to Venice.

Veteran Sub

for Bill Coyle

His number might get called at any second,
The coaches said, implying, "Be prepared . . .
Or else!" *Two* kinds of scouts now to be reckoned
With, and the words have left him slightly scared.
There isn't much that lies ahead of him,
And less than nothing he has left behind
In stats whose luster long ago grew dim.
His status wildly concentrates his mind.
Until he sees that if he takes the court
And blows this one last chance, they'll try to send
Him down, or ship him out, or shop him to
Some last-place team. He knows now what to do,
Considering that what has reached its end
Won't even lead the six o'clock report.

Watch City

Waltham, Massachusetts

Now, twice a day, it tells that timeless joke
By being right. When was it that it broke?
Some day long gone, but clearly, one-oh-one.
The frozen hands point out both moon and sun,
Both cloud and star. How long since it last struck
With its collected strength? Before it stuck,
Did people go about the morning town
Eager to hear their quarter-hours tossed down,
Or cursing their bad luck when they were late
For their appointments — even if with fate?
And did they grieve that day they lost their crier,
Silenced in the steeple's jutting spire?
Despite the prayers of those who hope it will,
The tower bells no answers, standing still.

What Was Left

The Pulitzer; *that* play; the goddess-star;
His day in the committee room; and then,
When it was born, the beaming pride in PEN
(One wonders if he lit a blunt cigar):
All these, they say, are signs, if any are,
Of fearless noble public purity.
But of the boy he called "the mongoloid"
In private (no one of his public knew),
And of the place that son was put away,
(A Titicut he managed to avoid
For forty years)? Well, what is there to say?
Right thinking offered little surety
That when he died the state would not pursue
His heir for every cent. Someone must pay.

Winter Exercises

Like mortars firing shells in flaking streams,
The barrels shooting snow in arcing beams
All down the fairway now have found their range.
They lay the white stuff down in soft exchange
For greens gone brown, until the summer course,
Surrendering its flags at last, invites
Fresh, dedicated tracks. Beneath the lights
Or in the sun, they're out in earnest force —
Parkas, sweaters, sliding from hole to hole,
Their gliding rigorous, their goal to get
Across without a spill, of course, and yet . . .
Why do the small deserters, pole by pole,
Fall back, fan out, and signal to the sky
That they need not be rescued where they lie?

The Author

Len Krisak has taught at Brandeis University, Northeastern University, and Stonehill College. His two chapbooks, *Midland* and *Fugitive Child*, came out in 1999 from Somers Rocks Press and Aralia Press, respectively. In 2000, his full-length collection *Even as We Speak* won the Richard Wilbur Prize and was published by the University of Evansville Press. In 2004, *If Anything* appeared from WordTech Editions; in 2006, Carcanet published his *Odes of Horace*, a complete translation; and in 2010 his complete translation of Virgil's *Eclogues* was published by the University of Pennsylvania Press. In 2014, his complete translation of Ovid's *Amores* and *Ars Amatoria* will appear from the University of Pennsylvania Press, his complete *Catullus* from Carcanet Press, and in 2015, his complete translation of Rilke's *Neue Gedichte* (New Poems) will be published by Boydell & Brewer.

In addition to the Richard Wilbur Prize, he has received the Robert Penn Warren and Robert Frost Prizes, the Pinch Prize, a Los Angeles Poetry Festival Award, and numerous honors from the New England Poetry Club, which awarded *Even as We Speak* the Motton Book Prize.

He is the former winner of the GoldPocket.com National Trivia Competition and is a four-time Champion on *Jeopardy*!

www.ingramcontent.com/pod-product-compliance
Lightning Source LLC
Chambersburg PA
CBHW031358160426
42813CB00090B/3260/J